PIERCED BY A RAY OF SUN

Other Poetry Anthologies by Ruth Gordon

PIERCED BY A RAY OF SUN

POEMS ABOUT THE TIMES WE FEEL ALONE

Selected by RUTH GORDON

HarperCollins*Publishers*

Library of Congress Cataloging-in-Publication Data
Gordon, Ruth.
    Pierced by a ray of sun : poems about the times we feel alone / selected by Ruth Gordon.
        p.   cm.
    Summary: An international anthology of poems about loneliness.
    Includes index.
    ISBN 0-06-023613-2. — ISBN 0-06-023614-0 (lib. bdg.)
    1. Young adult poetry.   2. Loneliness—Juvenile poetry.   [1. Poetry—Collections.   2. Loneliness—
Poetry.]   I. Gordon, Ruth, date.
PN6109.97.P54   1995   94-3757
808.81′9353—dc20   CIP
                                                                                                                       AC

Typography by Tom Starace
1   2   3   4   5   6   7   8   9   10
❖
First Edition

Acknowledgments

Every effort has been made to trace the ownership of all copyrighted material and to secure the necessary permission to reprint these selections. In the event of any question arising as to the use of any material, the editor and the publisher, while expressing regret for any inadvertent error, will be happy to make the correction in future printings. Thanks are due to the following for permission to reprint the copyrighted material listed below:

Aal, Katharyn Machan: "Pockets" from *Anthology of Magazine Verse & Yearbook of American Poetry*, 1986–1988 Edition. Copyright © Monitor Book Company, 1988.

Aguero, Kathleen: "Beating Up Billy Murphy in Fifth Grade," reprinted from *The Real Weather*, © 1987 by Kathleen Aguero, by permission of Hanging Loose Press and Kathleen Aguero.

Aiken, Joan: "Outing" by Joan Aiken, from *The Skin Spinners: Poems* by Joan Aiken. Copyright © 1976 by Joan Aiken. Reprinted by permission of Brandt & Brandt Literary Agents, Inc.

Anonymous: "On Education," from *Scholastic Scope* magazine, reprinted by permission of Scholastic, Inc.

Antler: "Raising My Hand" from *Last Words* by Antler, © 1986 by Antler (Ballantine), reprinted by permission of Antler.

Baber, Bob Henry: "handicaps" from *Pine Mountain Sand and Gravel*, copyright © 1985, reprinted with permission from Bob Henry Baber.

Balazs, Mary: "Pregnant Teenager on the Beach" from *Anthology of Magazine Verse & Yearbook of American Poetry*. Copyright © Monitor Book Company, 1980.

Boisseau, Michelle: "Eavesdropping" reprinted from *No Private Life*, Vanderbilt University Press, 1990; and from *Anthology of Magazine Verse & Yearbook of American Poetry*, 1984 Edition. Copyright © 1984 Monitor Book Company.

Ch'ien T'ao: "Written at a Party Where My Lord Gave Away a Thousand Bolts of Silk" translated by Kenneth Rexroth. Kenneth Rexroth: *Women Poets of China*. Copyright © 1972 by Kenneth Rexroth and Ling Chung. Reprinted by permission of New Directions Publishing Corp.

Cording, Robert: "Elegy for John, My Student Dead of AIDS" from *Anthology of Magazine Verse & Yearbook of American Poetry*, 1986–1988 Edition. Copyright © Monitor Book Company, 1988.

Cornish, Sam: "Fannie Lou Hamer" from *An Ear to the Ground* ed. by Marie Harris and Kathleen Aguero, copyright © 1989, reprinted with permission from Sam Cornish.

Dickinson, Emily: "341 (After great pain, a formal feeling comes)" from *The Complete Poems of Emily Dickinson* edited by Thomas H. Johnson. Copyright © 1929, 1935 by Martha Dickinson Bianchi; Copyright © renewed 1957, 1963 by Mary L. Hampson. Reprinted by permission of Little, Brown & Company, and also reprinted by the permission of the publishers and the Trustees of Amherst College from *The Poems of Emily Dickinson*, Thomas H. Johnson, ed., Cambridge, Mass.: The Belknap Press of Harvard University Press, Copyright © 1951, 1955, 1983 by the President and Fellows of Harvard College.

Divakaruni, Chitra Banerjee: "Yuba City School" by Chitra Banerjee Divakaruni is reprinted by permission of the publisher from *Black Candle* © C. B. Divakaruni (Calyx Books, 1991).

Dobyns, Stephen: "Fear" copyright © 1980 by Stephen Dobyns, from *Velocities* by Stephen Dobyns. Used by permission of Penguin, a division of Penguin Books USA Inc.

Espaillat, Rhina: "You Call Me by Old Names" from *Lapsing to Grace*, published by Bennett & Kitchel, P.O. Box 4422, East Lansing, MI, 48826. Reprinted by permission of Bennett & Kitchel.

Follain, Jean: "Dog With Schoolboys" translated by Keith Waldrop, from *The Random House Book of Twentieth-Century French Poetry* edited by Paul Auster (Random House, 1984), reprinted with permission from Keith Waldrop and the French publisher, Editions Gallimard.

Fortini, Franco: "To Friends" from *New Italian Poetry 1945 to the Present, a Bilingual Anthology* edited by Lawrence Smith, University of California Press, © 1981, reprinted by permission of University of California Press.

Friel, James P.: "Revolutionary" from *Anthology of Magazine Verse & Yearbook of American Poetry*. Copyright © Monitor Book Company, 1985.

Fuertes, Gloria: "When I Hear Your Name" translated by Philip Levine, from *Anthology of Magazine Verse & Yearbook of American Poetry*. Copyright © Monitor Book Company, 1984.

Giudici, Giovanni: "You Ask Me What It Means" from *New Italian Poetry 1945 to the Present, a Bilingual Anthology* edited by Lawrence Smith, University of California Press, © 1981, reprinted by permission of University of California Press.

Hall, Jim: "Winter in Texas" from *Anthology of Magazine Verse & Yearbook of American Poetry*. Copyright © Monitor Book Company, 1988.

Henri, Adrian: "Adrian Henri's Talking After Christmas Blues" from *Collected Poems*

In memory of Marc,
To the nonathlete dying young:
O, such a golden youth was he
&
To his sisters,
Janet
Gigi
Robin
May they, and all of us, live golden lives

Contents

Ognuno sta solo sul cuor della terra
trafitto da un raggio di sole . . .

Each of us is alone on the heart of the earth
pierced by a ray of sun . . .

Salvatore Quasimodo (1901–1968)
from "And Suddenly It's Evening"
Translated from the Italian by Jack Revan

A Note to the Reader

"Am I the only such person on Earth?"

Few of us manage to go through life without feeling alone, different, alienated, and lost from time to time. This collection was put together with the thought that throughout time and history many have felt as we feel. If we realize that we are not the only such people on Earth, perhaps poets' words of the distant past and recent present will help us face not only our differences, but also our sameness. Loneliness in Chinese, Yiddish, Native American, Russian, Spanish, and a host of other tongues may sound different, but each carries an emotion shared by all. We who are "pierced by a ray of sun" should remember that we are also standing in its brightness.

PIERCED BY A RAY OF SUN

You Ask Me What It Means

You ask me what
the word alienation means:
it is to die from the moment of birth
in order to live in a master

who sells you—it is to hand over
the things you carry—power, love,
total hate—in order to find
sex, wine, a broken heart.

It means to live outside yourself
while you believe you reside within
because the wind you yield to
knocks you off your feet.

You can fight it, but one day
is a century of dissipation:
the things you give away never
return to you, their source.

Waiting is another life,
but there is no other time:
the time which is you disappears,
what remains isn't you at all.

Giovanni Giudici (1924–)
Translated from the Italian by Lawrence R. Smith

RAISING MY HAND

One of the first things we learn in school is
    if we know the answer to a question
We must raise our hand and be called on
    before we can speak.
How strange it seemed to me then,
    raising my hand to be called on,
How at first I just blurted out,
    but that was not permitted.

How often I knew the answer
And the teacher (knowing I knew)
Called on others I knew (and she knew)
    had it wrong!
How I'd stretch my arm
    as if it would break free
    and shoot through the roof
    like a rocket!
How I'd wave and groan and sigh,
Even hold up my aching arm
    with my other hand
Begging to be called on,
Please, *me*, I know the answer!
Almost leaping from my seat
    hoping to hear my name.

Twenty-nine now, alone in the wilds,
Seated on some rocky outcrop
    under all the stars,
I find myself raising my hand
    as I did in first grade
Mimicking the excitement
    and expectancy felt then,
No one calls on me
    but the wind.

Antler (1946–)

The One-Armed Boy

has taught himself to play catch
with the walls of his house.
With great effort has learned
to open jars, trap grasshoppers,
write in straight lines. Has,
over time, discovered how
not to hear his mother weeping,
or his father roaring drunk.
Has carefully trained himself
to deflect the cutting
comments of his schoolmates.
If only a saw had chewed it off!
Or some gigantic shark, as in
his recurring fantasies. If only
he hadn't been born like this.
And yet, near sleep, the arm
that never was reaches out,
touches something even the boy
can't name. Like rain at midnight
falling into a field of poppies, it
gently quickens his non-existent hand.

Joseph Hutchison (1902–1988)

My Parents

My parents kept me from children who were rough
Who threw words like stones and who wore torn clothes.
Their thighs showed through rags. They ran in the street
And climbed cliffs and stripped by the country streams.

I feared more than tigers their muscles like iron
Their jerking hands and their knees tight on my arms.
I feared the salt coarse pointing of those boys
Who copied my lisp behind me on the road.

They were lithe, they sprang out behind hedges
Like dogs to bark at my world. They threw mud
While I looked the other way, pretending to smile.
I longed to forgive them, but they never smiled.

Stephen Spender (1909–)

Day

I remember how I first saw my father
as somebody who didn't know
what to do with his life;
I was on my way to school,
saw him down the hall on the edge of the bed,
his slacks dark against the open sheets,
the t-shirt white against his brown skin.

He'd stopped. He held one shoe
with its laces dangling.
His head lowered, his chin almost
to his chest—I don't remember asking
was he all right, what's the matter?

That was thirty years ago.
Perhaps he'd had the first pain
and couldn't move. Maybe he'd lost a job,
or knew he'd stopped loving and couldn't leave.

We hardly talked. I never knew.
I think now of the things that make a man stare
at the floor, the wide field of sheets
behind him, how the tired bulk of flesh
will not put on the second shoe,
wants only peace, rest.

Dona Luongo Stein (1935–)

BEATING UP BILLY MURPHY IN FIFTH GRADE

Who knows how it started?
We were the same age, but he was smaller
with wrists you could snap like green beans,
veins that showed blue runners through his skin.
His scalp was something dead beneath his crewcut
and I hated his pipsqueak voice
his hanging around with us girls.

Then somehow he was face down on the pavement,
my fist banging his back.
When my girlfriends pulled me off,
he whined like a toy engine:
I had hurt his sunburn,
I would pay if he went to the doctor.

He was an orphan I thought I should be nice to.
His aunt was sending him to military school.
I was ashamed but still sickened
remembering his soft hands, his thin eyelashes,
the schoolgirl in him.

Kathleen Aguero (1949–)

ENVY

I envy.
     This secret
I have not revealed before.
I know
     there is somewhere a boy
whom I greatly envy.
I envy
     the way he fights;
I myself was never so guileless and bold.
I envy
     the way he laughs—
as a boy I could never laugh like that.
He always walks about with bumps and bruises;
I've always been better combed,
               intact.
He will not miss
     all those passages in books
I've missed.
     Here he is stronger too.
He will be more blunt and harshly honest,
forgiving no evil even if it does some good;
and where I'd dropped my pen:
         "It isn't worth it!"—
he'd assert:
    "It's worth it!"—
         and pick up the pen.
If he can't unravel a knot,
       he'll cut it through,
whereas I can neither unravel
       nor cut through.

Once he falls in love,
                    he won't fall out of it,
while I keep falling in
                    and out of love.
I'll hide my envy.
                    Start to smile.
I'll pretend to be a simple soul:
"Someone has to smile;
someone has to live in a different way . . ."
But much as I tried to persuade myself of this,
repeating:
                    "To each man his fate . . ."
I can't forget there is somewhere a boy
who will achieve far more
                    than I.

Yevgeny Yevtushenko (1933–)
Translated from the Russian by George Reavey

Birth Elegy VI

I've learned something:
nothing is fair, but
you can't change the rules.

Natalie Robins (1938–)

A Half Blade of Grass

Death is still far off
                and everything is so hard,
as if the way up is on rotted stairs.
Life is getting bitter,
                like overheated milk
with foam burned black.
They say to me, sighing:
                "Feel sorry for yourself,"
but I'll take a half blade of grass in my teeth
and already I'm more cheerful
                from this gift of the field—
from the sourness
                and from the bitterness.
I'll take a gentle bit
                in summer or in spring,
and I am made happy by this green trifle,
and my people
                must have taken pity on me in advance,
because they don't spoil me with pity.
If they smash my ribs smartly in a fight,
I consider
                that's how it's supposed to be.
They jab me in the back
                and don't understand—
why I'm not smiling.
In those who were pitied in childhood,
there is no strength,
                but pervasive weakness.
A half blade of grass in the teeth—
                there's my whole secret,
and in the earth still growing—
                there's a half blade of grass.

Yevgeny Yevtushenko (1933–)
Translated from the Russian by Albert C. Todd

A Telegram

A telegram arrived yesterday
   About my brother
      Wounded in Vietnam.
        Nothing else.
          Nothing about
            time or
              place.
                  Just a short apology.

My mother cried for Jesus
   My father fainted when he heard
      I had never seen him so scared.

We sat quietly,
   Trying to avoid the sadness
   Written on each of our faces.
   Thinking of my brother,

      Their son,
      Across the ocean

     In a war
        Brought home to our aching hearts.

At night
  I feel lonely
  with my father's silence

   and my mother's tears.

Nora Naranjo Morse (1953–)

MOTHER

I wish that I could talk with her again.
That's what I thought of when I thought of home,
Always supposing I had a home to come to.
If she were here, we'd warm the Chinese pot
To brew a jasmine-scented elixir,
And I would tell her how my life has been—
All the parts that don't make sense to me,
And she would let me talk until the parts
Fitted together.

That will never be.
She couldn't wait for me to come to her—
Ten years away. I couldn't wish for her
To wait, all blind and helpless as she was.
So now I have come home to emptiness:
No silly welcome-rhyme, no happy tears,
No eager questioning. No way to get
An answer to my questions. Silence fills
The rooms that once were vibrant with her song,
And all the things I wanted to talk out
With her are locked forever in my heart.

I wander through the rooms where she is not.
Alone I sit on the hassock by her chair,
And there, at last, I seem to hear her voice:
"You're a big girl now. You can work things out."

Bea Exner Liu (1907–)

FORGOTTEN

Mom came home one day
and said my father had died.
Her eyes all red.
Crying for some stranger.
Couldn't think of anything to do,
so I walked around Beaver
telling the kids
and feeling important.
Nobody else's dad had died.
But then
nobody else's dad had worn
red-striped pajamas
and nobody else's dad had made
stuffed animals talk
and nobody else's dad had gone away
nine years ago.
Nobody else's dad had been so loved
by a four-year-old.
And so forgotten by one
now
thirteen.

Cynthia Rylant (1954–)

THE BLUE BOWL

Like primitives we buried the cat
with his bowl. Bare-handed
we scraped sand and gravel
back into the hole.
                    They fell with a hiss
and thud on his side,
on his long red fur, the white feathers
between his toes, and his
long, not to say aquiline, nose.

We stood and brushed each other off.
There are sorrows keener than these.

Silent the rest of the day, we worked,
ate, stared, and slept. It stormed
all night; now it clears, and a robin
burbles from a dripping bush
like the neighbor who means well
but always says the wrong thing.

Jane Kenyon (1947–)

Winter in Texas

A neighbor boy rings the doorbell
and asks if I have seen his black
Labrador. I have been reading Thirteenth
Century anonymous poetry and am thinking
of writing something about winter in Texas.
I stand in the doorway, holding my book
and a small notebook and a pen and I ask
the boy how long the dog has been gone,
what it looks like its name. He tells me
and there is anguish in his face and he is
anxious to get on to the next door.
Most of the poems I have been reading are
about loss. A young man has lost his loved
one, someone else has lost his illusions
of immortality. Another sees the swirling
leaves as a kind of loss. I see the boy
from the window by my chair, going from
house to house. I hear him singing out his
dog's name between the houses. These six-
hundred-year-old poems still have their pangs.
Together they have made me recall my own
losses. I look out at the barren branches
of an anonymous tree across the street.
Beneath the earth I know its roots branch down
into a mirror replica of the tree; I know
that what we see above the earth is only half
the truth. I have a dog myself and I can imagine
its loss. I was a boy once, and once had a dog
which vanished into a neighborhood, and I sang
out its name over and over. I have knocked on

strangers' doors. Normally, I bury sadnesses
like this one. It is the Twentieth Century,
I have a name, it is winter in Texas. This
feeling won't survive. It will swirl away like
all the others. A boy's voice sings out all
through the neighborhood the name of his loss.

Jim Hall (20th century)

Dog With Schoolboys

For fun the schoolboys crack the ice
along a path
next to the railroad
they are heavily clothed
in dark old woolens
belted with beat leather
The dog that follows them
no longer has a bowl to eat from
he is old
for he is their age.

Jean Follain (1903–1971)
Translated from the French by Keith Waldrop

CHILDHOOD

It would be good to give much thought, before
you try to find words for something so lost,
for those long childhood afternoons you knew
vanished so completely—and why?

We're still reminded—: sometimes by a rain,
but we can no longer say what it means;
life was never again so filled with meeting,
with reunion and with passing on

as back then, when nothing happened to us
except what happens to things and creatures:
we lived their world as something human,
and became filled to the brim with figures.

And became as lonely as a shepherd
and as overburdened by vast distances,
and summoned and stirred as from far away,
and slowly, like a long new thread,
introduced into that picture-sequence
where now having to go on bewilders us.

Rainer Maria Rilke (1875–1926)
Translated from the German by Edward Snow

NOBODY WAITS . . .

Nobody waits at the foot of the stairs any more
Or takes our hand crossing a street, the way they did
When we were young. Nobody tells us about the mean
Ant and the Grasshopper. Or teaches us to believe in God.

Nowadays nobody thinks
They all have enough just
So we have to live as they do—but alone . . .
(Impotent, dishonest, and inept.)

Anatoly Steiger (1907–1944)
Translated from the Russian by Paul Schmidt

LIES

Lying to the young is wrong.
Proving to them that lies are true is wrong.
Telling them
                that God's in his heaven
and all's well with the world
                                is wrong.
They know what you mean.
                            They are people too.
Tell them the difficulties
                can't be counted,
and let them see
                not only
                        what will be
but see
        with clarity
                these present times.
Say obstacles exist they must encounter,
sorrow comes,
                hardship happens.
The hell with it.
                Who never knew
the price of happiness
                will not be happy.
Forgive no error
                you recognize,
it will repeat itself,
                a hundredfold
and afterward
                our pupils
will not forgive in us
                what we forgave.

Yevgeny Yevtushenko (1933–)
Translated from the Russian by Robin Milner-Gulland and Peter Levi

Untitled

I shout 'I'm my own man'
Then 'I'm my own victim'
Smart banal games! Love, help me
Choose not to choose.

Rumi (1207–1273)
Translated from the Persian by Andrew Harvey

FEAR

His life frightened him. The sun in the sky,
the man next door—they all frightened him.
Fear became a brown dog that followed him home.
Instead of driving it away, he became its friend.
The brown dog named fear followed him everywhere.
When he looked in the mirror, he saw it under
his reflection. When he talked to strangers,
he heard it growl in their voices. He had a wife:
fear chased her away. He had several friends:
fear drove them from his home. The dog fear
fed upon his heart. He was too frightened
to die, too frightened to leave the house.
Fear gnawed a cave in his chest where it
shivered and whined in the night. Wherever
he went, the dog found him, until he became
no more than a bone in its mouth, until fear
fixed its collar around his throat, fixed
its leash to the collar. The dog named fear
became the only creature he could count on.
He learned to fetch the sticks it threw for him,
eat at the dish fear filled for him. See him
on the street, seemingly lost, nose pressed
against the heel of fear. See him in his backyard,
barking at the moon. It is his own face he
finds there, hopeless and afraid, and he leaps at it,
over and over, biting and rending the night air.

Stephen Dobyns (1941–)

On Education

He always wanted to explain things,
But no one cared.
So he drew.
Sometimes he would draw,
and it wasn't anything.
He wanted to carve it in stone
or write it in the sky,
and it would be only him and the sky and
the things inside him that needed saying.
It was after that he drew the picture.
It was a beautiful picture.
He kept it under his pillow
and would let no one see it.
He would look at it every night
and think about it.

When he started school,
he brought it with him, not to show anyone,
just to have along like a friend.
It was funny about school.
He sat at a square, brown desk,
like all the other square, brown desks.
He thought it should be red.
And his room was a square, brown room,
like all the other rooms.
It was tight and close and stiff.
He hated to hold the pencil and chalk,
his arms stiff, his feet flat on the floor,
stiff,
the teacher watching and watching.
The teacher came and spoke to him.

She told him to wear a tie
like all the other boys.
He said he didn't like them.
She said it didn't matter!
After that, they drew.
He drew all yellow.
It was the way he felt about morning,
and it was beautiful.
The teacher came and smiled at him.
"What's this?" she said. "Why don't you
draw something like Ken's drawing?
Isn't that beautiful?"
After that, his mother bought him a tie,
and he always drew airplanes and rocketships
like everyone else.
And he threw the old picture away.
And when he lay alone looking at the sky,
it was big and blue and all of everything,
but he wasn't anymore.
He was square inside and brown,
and his hands were stiff.
He was like everyone else.
The things inside that needed saying
didn't need it anymore.
It had stopped pushing.
It was crushed.
Stiff.
Like everything else.

Anonymous

Silent, but . . .

I may be silent, but
I'm thinking.
I may not talk, but
Don't mistake me for a wall.

Shigeji Tsuboi (1898–1975)
Translated from the Japanese by Geoffrey Bownas and Anthony Thwaite

DITCHED

A first grader
A federal boarding school
Pipestone
Said anin to the
first grown up
Got an icy blue-eyed stare
in return
Got a beating from a
second grader for crying
about the stare
Couldn't tell ma or dad
both were 300 miles away
Couldn't write, didn't know how
Couldn't mail, didn't know how
Runaway, got caught
Got an icy blue stare
and a beating
Got another beating
from a second grader
for crying about
the blue-eyed beating
Institutionalized
Toughed it out
Survived

Jim Northrup (1943–   )

anin = hello

HANDICAPS

With their stares others tell me
what I already know to be the truth:
my features do not conform
to the conventions of beauty or grace
When I hurry across Capital
with its unforgiving light
my feet and arms fail me,
and when I speak
my thoughts, though clear,
are slush as much as ice—
Still I say the difference between us
is only that of form.
You see, I too scan storefront windows
to verify I exist;
I too am stunned by the polluted sunset
like a gash in skyscraper glass;
I too hear the churchbells
ringing in the early orange dusk;
I envy youth its poetry
and its unrelenting lust

and my breath, like yours—
warm, humid, and grey—
lifts from deep within my lungs
pauses in December air
and evaporates
      as we all must
    in our sad anointed time
    in our difference of like, not kind

Bob Henry Baber (1950–)

Visiting Day, Worcester County House of Correction

I am a good girl, I have come directly
from my Ancient Greek class for a visit;
I have brought the shoes you wrote for; although

I am afraid of the high spiked fence,
towers around the walled yard, and the beefy
guards staring at my spring dress blown against

my thighs, I walk from the yard filled with
daffodils, hyacinths, and sculptured bushes
into the prison. I imagine your

brown eyes filled with patience as you wait while
one door is unlocked then locked behind you:
they bring you to me. You are not in a striped

uniform but wear a gray work suit. You
are as neat as you always were at home;
hair trimmed, face absolutely clean-shaven,

and nails their neat half-moons. I look at
everything but your eyes while you talk.
You have become a tape recording: you

ask where my mother goes, and when, then call
her a whore. Quickly I hand over
the shiny black shoes; I cannot look at
your eyes, they are not yours, Father.

Dona Luongo Stein (1935–)

29

NOVELLA

Two people in a room, speaking harshly.
One gets up, goes out to walk.
(That is the man.)
The other goes into the next room
and washes the dishes, cracking one.
(That is the woman.)
It gets dark outside.
The children quarrel in the attic.
She has no blood left in her heart.
The man comes back to a dark house.
The only light is in the attic.
He has forgotten his key.
He rings at his own door
and hears sobbing on the stairs.
The lights go on in the house.
The door closes behind him.
Outside, separate as minds,
the stars too come alight.

Adrienne Rich (1929–)

EAVESDROPPING

It was Mrs. Garvin, the doctor's wife,
who told my mother, Well, if you're that broke,
put the kids up for adoption.
Out under the porch light that summer,
we slapped at mosquitoes and invented
our brave escape—luminous sheets
knotted out the window
were the lines of a highway down the house.
We would know the way,
like ingenious animals, to go
quietly toward the river,
but we could imagine no further
than the shacks on stilts
shivering the water,
the Kentucky hills on the other side.
Denise, the youngest, took to sleepwalking
wading room to room for the place
one of us—curled up in a bed's corner—
might have left her. I'd wake
to her face pressed against my back
her hands reining the edges of my nightgown.
I didn't tuck her into my shoulder
but loosened her fingers and led her
back to her own bed, her fear
already seeping into me like water
or like the light spilling
from the milk truck
as it backfired down the street.

Michelle Boisseau (1955–)

CHILDREN OF THE MAFIOSI

are
sometimes like you were;
have Christmas and Grandma
torrone and lasagna
birthdays with favorite cousins,
and nightmares.

children of the mafiosi
are not sure what daddy does,
although it's important
and secret.
sometimes mamma cries
and we go away suddenly at night.

sometimes strangers come into the kitchen
where dad's home during the day cooking;
they don't take hats or coats off but sit
at the kitchen table with coffee and we are introduced then
pushed out of the room.

when police come to the door
we are polite and innocent
for we are older and we know
what dad does, where he goes when he's not home for a long
                                        long time.

the children of the mafiosi
grow up. we become nurses,
real estate agents, cops, teachers, secretaries,
social workers, engineers, truck drivers, and have families too;

                                                                          most

of us do not carry on our father's business,
never visit the penitentiary again,
do not carry guns in our suitcases,
do not drive white cadillacs;
we do not ask mother what it was like.

at night, for children of the mafiosi,
pillows explode like car engines, women are followed by men who
work with knives, then we wait under the sheets
listening for daylight
when we are honest,
eager to please, responsible,
us children of the mafiosi.

Dona Luongo Stein (1935–)

HOMEWORK

There are electric lights, thermostats,
television sets, and gas stoves; I sit
at the oilclothed table in the kitchen
doing homework. It is autumn
and I'd rather be picking grapes
for the jam my mother has said
she will make. I know without

being told I must do homework
first, since this evening I must
take care of my brothers and sisters
and help with the dishes. My mother
sighs, but she is going to her
stenography course in the city anyway.
My father hasn't been home for
weeks. I say nothing about their lives.
I am thirteen and daydream over
Latin and algebra. I think I am smart.
I'm sure my life will be different.

Dona Luongo Stein (1935–)

Ten Yen Coin

With his last ten yen coin
the boy wanted to make a phone call.
He wanted to talk to someone close
    in a rowdy language,
but none of his friends had telephones.
The ten yen coin was wet in his palm
and smelled of metal.
(Why should I buy gum?
    This ten yen coin will be used
        for something more important.)
Then the boy saw the car,
a haughty car like a beautiful woman,
a fierce car like an unreachable happiness . . .
and before he knew it himself,
the boy, taking the ten yen coin in his hand,
    cut into that beautiful finish,
a long deep gash—
Then the boy threw the ten yen coin,
with all his might,
    into the city's congestion.

Shuntarō Tanikawa (1931–)
Translated from the Japanese by Harold Wright

POCKETS

Walking down the street she finds her hands
jammed into pockets, blue jeans tight
across the hips she likes to move to music—
barefoot, hair down, silver tape recorder

blaring loud. She's seventeen. Her mother
calls her Bluebell just to get a rise, goes off
to work the morning shift in almost white
shoes and cap and apron, while daughter

slouches over Cheerios, sips coffee, stares ahead
and thinks how much she hates the smell of books.
"Goodbye." And once again "Goodbye" as now she
turns a corner stained with leaf tattoos

from early rain, pretends she doesn't care
that she is pregnant from a skinny man
she slept with once, who'll never know, who
thinks of her as something he once tasted,

might again. She moves along, indifferent
to the aching bit of smoke from cigarette
she sucks. She's seventeen. All's possible. All isn't.
Today at school they'll see a stupid film.

Katharyn Machan Aal (1952–)

Pregnant Teenager on the Beach

From her pool in the muddy shallows
she squints sixty yards out
at the white blister of the sunning deck.
On the diving board
a girl her own age shrieks,
topples with a bronzed youth
into the green water.
Separately they rise, an arc of light
like a rapier between them.
Laughing,
their glances fence,

lock.

Before her, in water low as their knees,
a circle of mothers
tow children on inflated plastic ducks,
sprinkle the murky water
over their sun-burned thighs.
She looks into their eyes:
can they remember a night
when the stars rose like a host
in the spring sky?

She stares at her abdomen
where beneath the tight skin
a sea churns,
alive with that small fish
whose gills prepare for the barbed air.
A heavy wave pulls her to shore,
drops her among stones

and cracked shells.

Mary Balazs (1939–)

When I Hear Your Name

When I hear your name
I feel a little robbed of it;
it seems unbelievable
that half a dozen letters could say so much.

My compulsion is to blast down every wall with your name.
I'd paint it on all the houses,
there wouldn't be a well
I hadn't leaned into
to shout your name there,
nor a stone mountain
where I hadn't uttered
those six separate letters
that are echoed back.

My compulsion is
to teach the birds to sing it,
to teach the fish to drink it,
to teach men that there is nothing
like the madness of repeating your name.

My compulsion is to forget altogether
the other 22 letters, all the numbers,
the books I've read, the poems I've written.
To say hello with your name.
To beg bread with your name.
"She always says the same thing," they'd say when they saw me,
and I'd be so proud, so happy, so self-contained.

And I'll go to the other world with your name on my tongue,
and all their questions I'll answer with your name
—the judges and saints will understand nothing—
God will sentence me to repeating it endlessly and forever.

Gloria Fuertes (1918–)

Translated from the Spanish by Ada Long and Philip Levine

GONE

Everybody loved Chick Lorimer in our town.
>   Far off
>   Everybody loved her.
So we all love a wild girl keeping a hold
>   On a dream she wants.
Nobody knows now where Chick Lorimer went.
Nobody knows why she packed her trunk . . . a few old things
And is gone,
>   Gone with her little chin
>   Thrust ahead of her
>   And her soft hair blowing careless
>   From under a wide hat,
Dancer, singer, a laughing passionate lover.

Were there ten men or a hundred hunting Chick?
Were there five men or fifty with aching hearts?
>   Everybody loved Chick Lorimer.
>   Nobody knows where she's gone.

Carl Sandburg (1878–1967)

UNTITLED

I lost my world, my fame, my mind—
The Sun appeared, and all the shadows ran.
I ran after them, but vanished as I ran—
Light ran after me and hunted me down.

Rumi (1207–1273)
Translated from the Persian by Andrew Harvey

Adrian Henri's Talking After Christmas Blues

Well I woke up this mornin' it was Christmas Day
And the birds were singing the night away
I saw my stocking lying on the chair
Looked right to the bottom but you weren't there
there was

        apples
           oranges
              chocolates
              . . . . aftershave
—but no you.

So I went downstairs and the dinner was fine
There was pudding and turkey and lots of wine
And I pulled those crackers with a laughing face
Till I saw there was no one in your place
there was

        mincepies
          brandy
            nuts and raisins
              . . . . mashed potato
—but no you.

Now it's New Year and it's Auld Lang Syne
And it's 12 o'clock and I'm feeling fine
Should Auld Acquaintance be Forgot?
I don't know girl, but it hurts a lot

there was

        whisky
          vodka
             dry Martini (stirred
                but not shaken)
. . . . and 12 New Year resolutions
—all of them about you.

So it's all the best for the year ahead
As I stagger upstairs and into bed
Then I looked at the pillow by my side
. . . . I tell you baby I almost cried
there'll be

        Autumn
        Summer
          Spring
            . . . . and Winter
—all of them without you.

Adrian Henri (1932–)

The Face of a Horse

Animals never sleep. At night when it's dark
They stand like a stone wall over the world.

A cow's sloping head has smooth horns
And makes noise in the straw; holding
Primaeval cheekbones separate,
The heavy stony forehead presses down
To inarticulate eyes
That barely can roll in circles.

But the face of a horse is sharp and fine.
He hears the talk of leaf and stone.
He listens! He knows the cries of animals,
From the ragged woods, the nightingale's call.

And being so wise, whom should he tell
All the miraculous things he knows?
The night is deep, constellations
Are lifting over the dark skyline.
And the horse is calmly standing guard,
The wind rustling his silky hair,
Each of his eyes like a huge burning world,
His mane spread—royal purple.

And if a man could see
The magic face of a horse
He would rip out his own silly tongue
To give to the horse. The magic horse
Is the one who really deserves a tongue!

Then we would hear words.
Words as big as apples, thick
As honey or curds.
Words that have the thrust of fire,
That fly into the soul and there make light,
Like fire shining on the wretched objects
Of some poor hut. Words without death,
Words that let us sing.
But now the stable is empty
And the trees can no longer be seen.
Morning, the miser, has covered up the mountains
And opened the fields for work.
The horse, from his cage of shafts,
Drawing a covered cart,
Looks with the eyes of a prisoner
At the mysterious, unmoving earth.

Nikolay Zabolotsky (1903–1958)
Translated from the Russian by Bob Perelman and Kathy Lewis

The Night Is Dark

The night is dark
And I am blind,
From my hand the stick
Is torn by the wind.

Bare is my sack,
Empty my heart,
A burden are both,
A useless load.

I hear the touch
Of someone's hand:
I pray you allow me
To carry your load.

Together we go,
The world is black:
I carry the sack
And he . . . my heart.

H. Leivick (1888–1962)
Translated from the Yiddish by Meyer Schapiro

FRIENDSHIP

Where is he now, I wonder?
And what's his life like?
Don't let me sit by the door
Expecting a sudden knock:
He will never come back.

Was it to hurt me, or himself?
(Or maybe he was lucky.)

One dream remains—the thought of peace.
—Don't need friendship, all words are empty,
And that word's the emptiest of all.

(For friendship you need to have two.
I was one, the other was air: you.)

Anatoly Steiger (1907–1944)
Translated from the Russian by Paul Schmidt

Elegy for John, My Student Dead of AIDS

In my office, where you sat years ago and talked
Of Donne, of how you loved
His persona, the bravado he could muster
To cover love's uncertainties,
Books still line the shelves, centuries
Of writers who've tried to make a kind of sense
Of life and death and, failing that,
Found words to stand at least
Against the griefs we can't resolve.

Now you're dead. And what I've got to say
Comes now from that silence
When our talk last fouled up. I allowed you less,
As always, than you wanted to say.
We talked beside the Charles, a lunch hour reunion
Of sorts after years of your postcards
(New York, San Francisco, Greece),
Failed attempts to find a place to live.
The warm weather had come on

In a rush. You talked of being the first born,
Dark-haired, Italian son. How you rarely visited
The family you so clearly loved.
I shifted to books, to sunlight falling
Through sycamores and the idle play of underlying
Shadows. When we parted,
All that was really left was the feeling
You deserved better. And yet I was relieved
Our hour was up, that we had kept your confusion

To yourself. We shook hands, you drove off to Boston.
Now you're dead, and I wonder
If your nobleness of living with no one
To turn to ended in dishonor,
Your family ashamed. Or if your death had
About it a frail dignity,
Each darkening bruise precise as a writer's word,
Saying, at last, who you were—exactly
And to anyone who would listen.

Robert Cording (1949-)

UNTITLED

After great pain, a formal feeling comes—
The Nerves sit ceremonious, like Tombs—
The stiff Heart questions was it He, that bore,
And Yesterday, or Centuries before?

The Feet, mechanical, go round—
Of Ground, or Air, or Ought—
A Wooden way
Regardless grown,
A Quartz contentment, like a stone—

This is the Hour of Lead—
Remembered, if outlived,
As Freezing persons, recollect the Snow—
First—Chill—then Stupor—then the letting go—

Emily Dickinson (1830–1886)

from In Memoriam A.H.H.

VII

Dark house, by which once more I stand
   Here in the long unlovely street,
   Doors, where my heart was used to beat
So quickly, waiting for a hand,

A hand that can be clasp'd no more—
   Behold me, for I cannot sleep,
   And like a guilty thing I creep
At earliest morning to the door.

He is not here; but far away
   The noise of life begins again,
   And ghastly thro' the drizzling rain
On the bald street breaks the blank day.

Alfred, Lord Tennyson (1809–1892)

ABSENCE

It was always there,
The great white pine,
Shelter and solid comfort.
From the second floor
I could watch red squirrels
Play, nuthatches lead
Their compulsive lives
In its ample branches.

From the third floor
I could turn away
From the glittering ocean
And rest my eyes
On the thick soft green.
In all seasons wind
Murmured through it.
It was always present.
We lived along together.

Until a winter hurricane
Brought it, shuddering,
Down against the house,
Until that quiet strength
Was broken by force.

On the second floor
The windows are empty
And here on the third
Ragged firs
And formless bits of sky
Are only an irritation.
The air is silent.

Must we lose what we love
To know how much we loved it?

It is always there now,
That absence, that awful absence.

May Sarton (1912–)

An Irish Airman Foresees His Death

I know that I shall meet my fate
Somewhere among the clouds above;
Those that I fight I do not hate,
Those that I guard I do not love;
My country is Kiltartan Cross,
My countrymen Kiltartan's poor,
No likely end could bring them loss
Or leave them happier than before.
Nor law, nor duty bade me fight,
Nor public men, nor cheering crowds,
A lonely impulse of delight
Drove to this tumult in the clouds;
I balanced all, brought all to mind,
The years to come seemed waste of breath,
A waste of breath the years behind
In balance with this life, this death.

William Butler Yeats (1865–1939)

Revolutionary

You cannot talk of violence
as you would
of putting the cat out at night
can you hear the skull cracking
flesh pouring over willing fingers
like blood
that is violence
revolution
beware of warriors
who plan their battles
in the sky
then go away
leave the earth
to die

how many bodies will be enough?
when will "justice" have drunk
full?

that man should live better
he must die

it puzzles me
it must be a new kind
of christianity
though Christ gave
his own life
now the air smells
of takers
too young
to ever have given

James P. Friel (1958–)

The Silence Now

These days the silence is immense.
It is there deep down, not to be escaped.
The twittering flight of goldfinches,
The three crows cawing in the distance
Only brush the surface of this silence
Full of mourning, the long drawn-out
Tug and sigh of waters never still—
The ocean out there, and the inner ocean.

Only animals comfort because they live
In the present and cannot drag us down
Into those caverns of memory full of loss.
They pay no attention to the thunder
Of distant waves. My dog's eager eyes
Watch me as I sit by the window, thinking.

At the bottom of the silence what lies in wait?
Is it love? Is it death? Too early or too late?
What is it I can have that I still want?

My swift response is to what cannot stay,
The dying daffodils, peonies on the way.
Iris just opening, lilac turning brown
In the immense silence where I live alone.

It is the transient that touches me, old,
Those light-shot clouds as the sky clears,
A passing glory can still move to tears,
Moments of pure joy like some fairy gold
Too evanescent to be kept or told.
And the cat's soft footfall on the stair
Keeps me alive, makes Nowhere into Here.
At the bottom of the silence it is she
Who speaks of an eternal Now to me.

May Sarton (1912–)

When I Have Fears

When I have fears that I may cease to be
   Before my pen has gleaned my teeming brain,
Before high-piled books, in charactery,
   Hold like rich garners the full ripened grain;
When I behold upon the night's starred face,
   Huge cloudy symbols of a high romance,
And think that I may never live to trace
   Their shadows, with the magic hand of chance;
And when I feel, fair creature of an hour,
   That I shall never look upon thee more,
Never have relish in the faery power
   Of unreflecting love;—then on the shore
Of the wide world I stand alone, and think
   Till love and fame to nothingness do sink.

John Keats (1795–1821)

END OF THE BEGINNING

Someone said we begin to die
the minute we're born.
Death is a part of life.
Who knows why the Creator
thins the herd.
Another old saying says
we must all be prepared
to give up those we love
or die first.
Take time to mourn.
Take time to remember.
Everything happens in cycles.
The pain you feel was once
balanced by someone's joy
when that baby was born.
The loss you feel today
will be replaced by good
long-lasting memories.
Is there a message here? Yah,
treat others like this
is your last day above ground.

Jim Northrup (1943–)

AIDS

We are stretched to meet a new dimension
Of love, a more demanding range
Where despair and hope must intertwine.
How grow to meet it? Intention
Here can neither move nor change
The raw truth. Death is on the line.
It comes to separate and estrange
Lover from lover in some reckless design.
Where do we go from here?

Fear.   Fear.   Fear.   Fear.

Our world has never been more stark
Or more in peril.
It is very lonely now in the dark
Lonely and sterile.

And yet in the simple turn of a head
Mercy lives. I heard it when someone said
"I must go now to a dying friend.
Every night at nine I tuck him into bed,
And give him a shot of morphine,"
And added, "I go where I have never been."
I saw he meant into a new discipline
He had not imagined before, and a new grace.

Every day now we meet it face to face
Every day now devotion is the test.
Through the long hours, the hard, caring nights
We are forging a new union. We are blest.

As closed hands open to each other
Closed lives open to strange tenderness.
We are learning the hard way how to mother.
Who says it is easy? But we have the power.
I watch the faces deepen all around me.
It is the time of change, the saving hour.
The word is not fear, the word we live,
But an old word suddenly made new,
As we learn it again, as we bring it alive:

Love.   Love.   Love.   Love.

May Sarton (1912–)

Untitled

"Hope" is the thing with feathers—
That perches in the soul—
And sings the tune without the words—
And never stops—at all—

And sweetest—in the Gale—is heard—
And sore must be the storm—
That could abash the little Bird
That kept so many warm—

I've heard it in the chillest land—
And on the strangest Sea—
Yet, never, in Extremity,
It asked a crumb—of Me.

Emily Dickinson (1830–1886)

Should I Tell of All the Absolute Fools

Should I tell of all the absolute fools,
Who hold the fate of mankind in their hands?

Should I tell of all the scoundrels who
Depart into history crowned with wreaths?

Should I—hell!
                    Under the bridges of Paris it's quiet
And why should I care how things turn out.

Georgy Ivanov (1894–1958)
Translated from the Russian by Daniel Weissbort

Outing

Every time I visit a strange town
I take my mother with me

I can feel her seeing through my eyes
gazing at shopwindows, longing to buy a book, a toy, a
    heavy glass jug
"Shall we go and look at the cathedral?" she says
I can hear her listening to two old ladies by the post office
"That one says local, that one says all other places"
"I can read, can't I? I was just taking me time. I can have a
    look, can't I?"

I can feel her wanting to comfort some crying child
wanting to get into conversation with some glum-looking man
and cheer him up
"Do let's go down that dear little street and see where it
    goes," she says
as often as not
it is a cul-de-sac, ending in a builder's yard
which only amuses her
I can feel her hoping there will be beautiful strange things in
    the shops
and a river with bridges and somebody playing the organ
in the cathedral
I can feel this active love
she had of doing and seeing
going and being
work in me like yeast as I walk new streets
not memory but an overlap
from her life to mine; not memory; you do not remember
what is still happening
I do not begin where she ended, for she has not ended

every time I visit a strange town and walk strange streets
I take her with me

Joan Aiken (1924–)

UNTITLED

We are lonely . . .
until we find ourselves.

Proverb

FANNIE LOU HAMER

fannie
lou
hamer
never
heard
of
in chicago
was known for
her
big
black
mouth
in the south
fannie lou
ate
her greens
watched
her land
and wanted
to
vote

men went
to the bottom
of the river
for wanting less
but fannie
got up
went to the courthouse

big as a fist
black as the ground
underfoot

Sam Cornish (1935–)

YOU CALL ME BY OLD NAMES

You call me by old names: how strange
to think of "family" and "blood,"
walking through flakes, up to the knees
in cold and democratic mud.

And suddenly I think of people
dead many centuries ago:
my ancestors, who never knew
the dubious miracle of snow. . . .

Don't say my names, you seem to mock
their charming, foolish, Old World touch—
Call me "immigrant," or Social
Security card such-and-such,
or future citizen, who boasts
two eyes, two ears, a nose, a mouth,
but no names from another life,
a long time back, a long way south.

Rhina Espaillat (1932–)

Prospective Immigrants
Please Note

Either you will
go through this door
or you will not go through.

If you go through
there is always the risk
of remembering your name.

Things look at you doubly
and you must look back
and let them happen.

If you do not go through
it is possible
to live worthily

to maintain your attitudes
to hold your position
to die bravely

but much will blind you,
much will evade you,
at what cost who knows?

The door itself
makes no promises.
It is only a door.

Adrienne Rich (1929–)

Katori Maru, October 1920

Two weeks across a strange sea
big waves, the ship
spilling its toilets.
People sick of the ocean
run from bulkhead to bulkhead,
trying to keep their balance
on the slick iron deck.

My mother asks herself in Japanese
why her older sister has to die,
why now she must marry the stranger
who speaks Japanese & English
and swears with the crew.
She thinks back to Nagano-ken,
pictures her mother
cracking a brown egg
over a bowl of rice
while her father washes raw soil
from his thick hands.
Today she could trade her future
for the bottom of the ocean.

Waves, floating waves,
rise above the railing,
drift out of sight. Vancouver Island
is a memory of home, hills
soft & green as crushed velvet.

In Tacoma, Minoru buys
Western clothes: pink taffeta dress
full of pleats, wide-brimmed hat,
white gloves, a leather handbag
and awkward high heels.

No more flowered silk,
obi sash and getas.
He brings out a used coat from the closet,
thick maroon wool, brown fur collar.
It is too full in the shoulders,
the size & color
fit her sister.
But for now she accepts it.
The rain feels heavy
on the gray sidewalks of America.

James Masao Mitsui (1940–)

RECIPE

Round Eyes

Ingredients: scissors, Scotch magic transparent tape,
            eyeliner—water based, black.
            Optional: false eyelashes.

Cleanse face thoroughly.

For best results, powder entire face, including eyelids.
    (lighter shades suited to total effect desired)

With scissors, cut magic tape 1/16" wide, 3/4"–1/2" long—
depending on length of eyelid.

Stick firmly onto mid-upper eyelid area
    (looking down into handmirror facilitates finding
    adequate surface)

If using false eyelashes, affix first on lid, folding any
excess lid over the base of eyelash with glue.

Paint black eyeliner on tape and entire lid.

Do not cry.

Janice Mirikitani (1942–)

PHOTOGRAPH OF A CHILD, JAPANESE-AMERICAN EVACUATION, BAINBRIDGE ISLAND, WASHINGTON, MARCH 30, 1942

The soft sound of his steps on the pier
is obscured by the heavy footfall

of the adults, rippling the planked deck.
One hand reaches above his head

to wrap around father's ring finger;
the other clutches a balsa model

of a U.S. fighter plane, held
upside down against his chest.

He is the only one who uses this time
to peer between the cracks at his feet,

trying to see the shiny ribs of water,
imagine a monstrous flounder hugging

the sediment, both eyes staring
from the top of its flat head.

James Masao Mitsui (1940–)

Destination: Tule Lake Relocation Center, May 20, 1942

She had raised the window
higher

than her head; then
paused

to lift wire spectacles,
wiping

sight back with a wrinkled
hand-

kerchief. She wanted to watch
the old

place until the train's passing
erased

the tarpaper walls and tin roof;
she had

been able to carry away
so little.

The finger of her left
hand

worried two strings
attached

to a baggage tag
flapping

from her
lapel.

James Masao Mitsui (1940–)

American Geisha

1.

There are people
who admire
the aesthetics
of our traditions.

And ask politely,
Where are you from?

Lodi
Minneapolis
Chicago
Gilroy
South Bend
Tule Lake
San Francisco
New York
L.A.

They persist and
ask again.

Compliment
our command of the
English language

2.

American white actress
plays the role
of white American Geisha

filmed on location
in Japan.

It was sooooo hard
says she
because American women walk

in strides

shaking it baby.

Over there,
no hips, no shaking,
point the toes inward and . . .
don't speak
unless spoken to.

Japanese women,
says she,
don't walk.

They place themselves
like art objects.

3.

Mr. Wong
went to Washington, D.C.
served on a Commission
for Small Business.
Was asked
if he was familiar
with the system of free enterprise?

and how come
he didn't speak
with an accent?

4.

They saw
I was Asian
and offered
to revise the program.

So I could read
my poetry
first.

I wouldn't want to follow
HIM.

He is very articulate.

5.

My daughter
was called
F. O. B.

at the beach

bosomed in her swimsuit.

Shake it baby, does it slide sideways?

6.

Do we say thank you?

when they tell us that they've
visited Japan
Hong Kong
Peking
Bali
Guam
Manila
several times

and it's so quaint
lovely
polite
exotic
hospitable
interesting

And when did we arrive?

Since we speak
English so well.

Janice Mirikitani (1942–)

Yuba City School

From the black trunk I shake out
my one American skirt, blue serge
that smells of mothballs. Again today
Neeraj came crying from school. All week
the teacher has made him sit
in the last row, next to the fat boy
who drools and mumbles,
picks at the spotted milk-blue
skin of his face, but knows
to pinch, sudden-sharp,
when she is not looking.

The books are full of black curves,
dots like the eggs the boll-weevil lays
each monsoon in furniture-cracks
in Ludhiana. Far up in front
the teacher makes word-sounds
Neeraj does not know. They float
from her mouth-cave, he says,
in discs, each a different color.

Candy-pink for the girls
in their lace dresses, marching
shiny shoes. Silk-yellow
for the boys beside them,
crisp blond hair, hands raised
in all the right answers. Behind them
the Mexicans, whose older brothers,
he tells me, carry knives,
whose catcalls and whizzing rubber bands
clash, mid-air, with the teacher's
voice, its sharp purple edge.

For him, the words are
a muddy red, flying low and heavy,
and always the one he has learned to understand:
idiot, idiot, idiot.

I heat the iron over the stove. Outside
evening blurs the shivering
in the eucalyptus. Neeraj's shadow
disappears into the hole
he is hollowing all afternoon.
The earth, he knows, is round, and if
one can tunnel all the way through,
he will end up in Punjab,
in his grandfather's mango orchard,
his grandmother's songs lighting
on his head, the old words
glowing like summer fireflies.

In the playground, Neeraj says,
invisible hands snatch at his uncut hair,
unseen feet trip him from behind,
and when he turns, ghost laughter
all around his bleeding knees.
He bites down on his lip
to keep in the crying. They are
waiting for him to open his mouth,
so they can steal his voice.

I test the iron with little drops of water
that sizzle and die. Press down
on the wrinkled cloth. The room fills
with a smell like singed flesh.

Tomorrow in my blue skirt I will go
to see the teacher, my tongue
stiff and swollen
in my unwilling mouth, my few
English phrases. She will pluck them
from me, nail shut my lips. My son
will keep sitting in the last row
among the red words that drink his voice.

Chitra Banerjee Divakaruni (1956–)

Note: The boy in the poem is a Sikh immigrant, whose religion
forbids the cutting of his hair. (Yuba City is in northern California.)

THAT MOUNTAIN FAR AWAY

My home over there, my home over there,
My home over there, now I remember it!
And when I see that mountain far away,
Why, then I weep. Alas! What can I do?
What can I do? Alas! What can I do?
My home over there, now I remember it.

Tewa

Translated from the Tewa by Herbert J. Spinden

Ngan Do in Grosse Pointe

Father arranged her
  stay with us
through Immigration.
  Yet, in a blue
month, she's shown
  no gratitude
for this country-
  club atmosphere.

Her face still wears
  the war in
Cambodia.
  Fire dreams of sons,
an ancient daughter,
  waken her, shaking,
afraid to break
  the imperial air.

A ravaged peasant,
  she looks Chinese,
speaks a bit of French,
  an old woman
at thirty-seven.
  Ebony eyes,
gossamer hair,
  her mouth, her sorrow.

Evenings, when the china
     & the children
have been cared for,
     she stares at the TV.
numbed to the guns,
     yet lit with a soft
expectancy, unaccustomed
     to continual laughter.
In time, she will own
     a house & house
cats & fashionable
     shoes & a face
the color of apricots &
     the view of the suburbs
that has no place
     for fire dreaming.

J. Patrick Lewis (1942–)

HEAVEN-HAVEN
(A NUN TAKES THE VEIL)

I have desired to go
   Where springs not fail,
To fields where flies no sharp and sided hail
   And a few lilies blow.

And I have asked to be
   Where no storms come,
Where the green swell is in the havens dumb,
   And out of the swing of the sea.

Gerard Manley Hopkins (1844–1889)

To Friends

It's getting late. I see you, just
like me in your weakness for emotion,
with overcoats, papers, sputtering
lamps, hair already thin,
with words and winks, excited

and depressed, wasted and yet children, hoarse
from uninterrupted conversation,
as you go down into this gray valley,
as you press down the stunned grass
where the way and the light by now are lost.

The voices I hear distant as the wires
beyond the mountains between rocks and hollows.
Every word that reaches me is farewell.
And I slow down my pace and follow you in my heart,
one here, one there, on the downward path.

Franco Fortini (1917–)
Translated from the Italian by Lawrence R. Smith

DEAR NEIGHBOR GOD

Dear neighbor God, if sometimes I disturb
you in the middle of the night with my knocking,
it's because so often I can't hear you breathing
and know: you're alone over there.
And if you need something, and no one's there
to fill the cup and put it in your fingers,
I'm always listening. Only say the word.
I'm right here.
Only a little wall stands between us,
built by chance: for this is all it might take—
one cry from your mouth or mine,
and it would break down
and not make a scene, or sound.

    It is made up of all your images.

And your images stand around you like names.
And if just once the light in me burns high
that shows the way to you from deep inside,
it goes to waste as glare spilling on their frames.

And my mind, so soon to stumble and go lame,
wanders away from you, homeless, exiled.

Rainer Maria Rilke (1875–1926)
Translated from the German by Steven Lautermilch

Last Apple

"I am like the last apple
That falls from the tree
and no one picks up."
I kneel to the fragrance
of the last apple,
and I pick it up.

In my hands—the tree,
in my hands—the leaf,
in my hands—the blossom,
and in my hands—the earth
that kisses the apple
that no one picks up.

Malka Heifetz Tussman (1896–1987)
Translated from the Yiddish by Marcia Falk

I Am A Rock

A winter day
In a deep and dark December;
I am alone,
Gazing from my window to the streets below
On a freshly fallen silent shroud of snow.
I Am A Rock,
I am an island.

I've built walls,
A fortress deep and mighty,
That none may penetrate.
I have no need of friendship;
        friendship causes pain.
It's laughter and it's loving I disdain.
I Am A Rock,
I am an island.

Don't talk of love,
But I've heard the words before;
It's sleeping in my memory.
I won't disturb the slumber of feelings
        that have died.
If I never loved I never would have cried.
I Am A Rock,
I am an island.

I have my books
And my poetry to protect me;
I am shielded in my armor,
Hiding in my room, safe within my womb.
I touch no one and no one touches me.
I Am A Rock,
I am an island.

And a rock feels no pain;
And an island never cries.

Paul Simon (1942–)

Written at a Party Where My Lord Gave Away a Thousand Bolts of Silk

A bolt of silk for each clear toned song.
Still these beauties do not think it is enough.
Little do they know of a weaving girl,
Sitting cold by her window,
Endlessly throwing her shuttle to and fro.

Ch'ien T'ao (early 11th century)
Translated from the Chinese by Kenneth Rexroth and Ling Chung

DOG

Sadder than myself
there is a dog
there—
down the alley
silent
cowering
only his eyes are wide open
nobody calls him
nobody notices him
when I am sad
sadder than myself,
there is a dog
always
there
beside me
never begging for pity,
merely
there.

Shuntarō Tanikawa (1931–)
Translated from the Japanese by Harold Wright

To the tune The Phoenix Hairpin

The world's love runs thin.
Human love turns evil.
Rain strips, in the yellow twilight,
The flowers from the branches.
The dawn wind will dry my tear stains.
I try to write down the trouble of my heart.
I can only speak obliquely, exhausted.
It is hard, hard,
We are each of us all alone.
Today is not yesterday.
My troubled mind sways
Like the rope of a swing.
A horn sounds in the cold depth of the night.
Afraid of people's questions,
I will swallow my tears
And pretend to be happy.
Deceit. Deceit. Deceit.

T'ang Wan (12th century)
Translated from the Chinese by Kenneth Rexroth and Ling Chung

Twenty Billion Light Years of Loneliness

Mankind on a little globe
Sleeps, awakes and works
Wishing at times to be friends with Mars.

Martians on a little globe
Are probably doing something; I don't know what
(Maybe *sleep-sleeping, wear-wearing,* or *fret-fretting*)
While wishing at times to be friends with Earth

This thing called universal gravitation
Is the power of loneliness pulling together.

The universe is distorted
So all join in desire.

The universe goes on expanding
So all feel uneasy.

At the loneliness of twenty billion light years
Without thinking, I sneezed.

Shuntarō Tanikawa (1931–)
Translated from the Japanese by Harold Wright

Indexes of Authors
Titles
First lines

Index of Authors

Index of Titles

Index of First Lines

I remember how I first saw my father 6
I shout 'I'm my own man' 22
I wish that I could talk with her again. 13
In my office, where you sat years ago and talked 48
It was always there, 52
It was Mrs. Garvin, the doctor's wife, 31
It would be good to give much thought, before 19
It's getting late. I see you, just 87
I've learned something: 10
Like primitives we buried the cat 15
Lying to the young is wrong. 21
Mankind on a little globe 95
Mom came home one day 14
My home over there, my home over there, 83
My parents kept me from children who were rough 5
Nobody waits at the foot of the stairs any more 20
One of the first things we learn in school is 2
Round Eyes 72
Sadder than myself 93
She had raised the window 74
Should I tell of all the absolute fools, 63
Someone said we begin to die 59
The night is dark 46
The one-armed boy has taught himself to play catch 4
The soft sound of his steps on the pier 73
The world's love runs thin. 94
There are electric lights, thermostats, 34
There are people 76
These days the silence is immense. 56

About the Anthologist

RUTH GORDON is a highly respected librarian, well known for her unflagging commitment to young people and her many contributions to the field of children's books.

She is the compiler of *Under All Silences: Shades of Love,* a collection of love poems that was chosen a Best Book of 1987 by both *School Library Journal* and the American Library Association, as well as being named one of the Best of the '80s by *Booklist.* She is also the compiler of two other poetry anthologies: *Time Is the Longest Distance* and *Peeling the Onion,* both of which received starred reviews in *Booklist.*

A native of Chicago, Ruth Gordon has lived in New York, Boston, Rhode Island, Italy, and for the last several years Sonoma County, California.